French Regards

by Bernard Cadillon

Bernard Cadillon

Original title
French Regards

Covers paintings
Bernard Cadillon

Cover design
Sonja Smolec

Layout & Edit
Sonja Smolec
Yossi Faybish

Published by
Aquillrelle

ISBN 978-1-4478-9252-6

avant-propos...

"Je sais que je ne sais rien" disait Socrate. Plus récemment Sacha Guitry pensait *"Le peu que je sais, c'est à mon ignorance que je le dois".*

Je ne peux pas vraiment affirmer être un autodidacte mais je ne suis pas un Pic de la Mirandole. Ce que j'ai appris, je l'ai appris au fur et à mesure à l'exemple du proverbe chinois *"Ne crains pas d'avancer lentement, crains seulement de t'arrêter"*, et sauf pendant des périodes de maladie, je ne me suis jamais arrêté d'écrire ou de dessiner, ce qui apportera sans doute au lecteur une vision large de ma production poétique.

Table of Contents

America

Las Vegas

You scramble
When you gamble.
You have a poker face
No smile, no trace
Of anger,
But your finger
Says danger
In a body language
And it is like a cage
That falls on your shoulder.
You mislead no one
With your old trap,
You are alone
With your road map
And you measure the gap
Between you and the younger.
You become an elder
For the game
That needs a big frame.
It's a shame.

AC/DC

Bernard Cadillon - *Powe*

Hyper Power

Mother nature,
Mother culture
Because of the link
Between brood
And food,
My ink
Sometimes bleeds
Thinking of the greed
Of those who do not heed
Neither the seed
Nor the reed
That they try to weed
Even if there is no need
At the highest speed
To protect their tweeds
With signed deeds,
While starving
Africans sell carving
Statues of their ancestors
In these times pastors.

Bernard Cadillon

Heimatlos

In Sedona,
Arizona,
What stays
Of the great painter :
A house with two storeys.
Vanished as in winter
His sculptures
In stone,
Strange figures
All gone.
The life in Paris
Was far in this new basis.
Maybe that he remembered the camps
In south of France,
Where they were as tramps
Him and others in no accordance
To their status
And in hiatus
With what was honest
Dear, dear Max Ernst.

JFK

John Fitzgerald Kennedy is born
In 1917 in Brookline, Massachussets
At eighteen, he integrates Princeton, but torn
Were his studies, but his assets
Promote him the year after
To Harvard, and later,
He visited the old continent
And wrote a thesis
On the british participation
In Munich, that was pertinent
And spread the hypothesis
That was sleeping Albion.
In 1941, he wanted to enroll
But he was invalided
Because of the disease of Adison,
But as he did not fear the roll,
He was finally incorporated
In the Navy and gained a medal
But in 1963, it was metal
That his brain perforated.

Pilgrimage

On the Mayflower, the new immigrants
Were not tenants,
Neither lieutenants,
Not all experimented,
And were not all quakers,
And certainly not fakers,
But they would have been quaked
If they had seen,
On the hills green,
Their heirs
Naked,
With long hairs,
Singing flower power
And let the sowers lower
In San Francisco,
California.
Long time ago before disco,
They watched movies psychedelic,
That hurt the ethic
And that cloud the cornea.

Terra Incognita

Like Magellan and Mercator,
Cristobal Colon was not a Spanish sailor.
He wanted to find a new path to India
And he discovered America,
With Nina, Pinta, Santa Maria,
Leaving old Europa,
Like one more
And Eric the Viking,
More than five hundred years before.
He entered in the History
Bringing a new territory
To his queen and his king,
Fernando and Isabel,
Each other catholic
That had fighted the Ismael
Believers, in great fever.
But he finished his career
Poor and alcoholic.

The Dove and the Falcon

In 1925, Pierre Salinger comes to the world.
His mother was French,
As frequently he told.
In 1957, he gave advice to the Kennedy branch.
In 1964, for California, he was named senator
That was not his first honor
In 1977, he became editor at ABC News, in Paris.
In 2000, he retired in France, near Valauris,
He is buried in USA at Arlington
In 2006, in France was inaugurated a museum
At his memory, very different to a Colosseum.
On the other hand
Vernon Walters was considered as a falcon
In Europe and people brand
His lack of leniency
Nevertheless to save American bacon,
He never hesitated to speak without deficiency
With what can be called enemies.
Till 1972, in Paris, he played a role with Vietnamese
In peace process, weaving ties.

The Son of the Wolf

Was born in 1876, John Griffith London
In San Francisco from Flora Wellman.
She married the same year to the father, John London,
A disabled civil war veteran.
Early in adulthood, he became Jack
To end with his life of stretcher and pack
Holder. But in 1897 he went to the Yukon
And began writing his first stories
Of which I will not make the inventories,
But far from the manners in Boston,
In 1903, "The call of the wild" was published
Surely one of his best productions
But no compliment had been fished.
He was maybe an alcoholic
But certainly not a catholic.
At 29, he built a ship "the Snark"
And went sailing. We park
In Pacific, after a 27 month trip on the bark;
He decided to sell the boat
And to be back in America with a new coat.

Bernard Cadillon - *Montagn*

Wall Street

You are not an American
You are an european,
Not sefarade, but ashkenaze
As your forefathers,
To remember the big blaze,
You speak Yiddish,
And even if you are youngish,
You speculate on the financial lathers,
At Wall Street and on other stock exchange places,
Running to achieve the races
Around the clocks.
You have a big wallet,
Full of addresses on all the blocks
Of the city and on the jet set,
That plays cricket,
Holding with both hands a mallet,
As of no commune
Origin and parentage,
You can imagine at your age
Touching the summit of the dune.

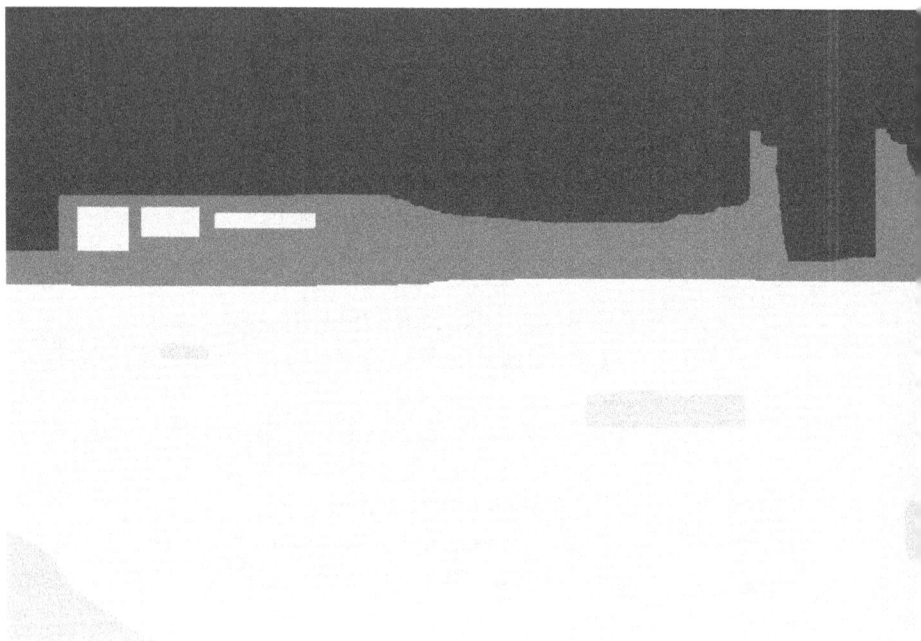

Bernard Cadillon - *Wood on wate*

Food for Flood

There is no good
Since the starting of the flood.
For all the inhabitants,
Modern immigrants,
The area is evacuated,
And a dead zone located,
Except for the militaries and the rescuers.
Long time before, the first refugees
Had found shelters
Roundabout in the other counties,
And at the border boundaries
With some red cross referees.
Nevertheless, float the cadavers
Along the rivers and the bayous
Sometimes stolen by some voyous,
And even if the mayor
Had a dignified behavior
We can say "Is it America,
Or Africa?
Jesus, my savior"

Casino

(variant of Las Vegas)

You scramble
When you gamble.
You have a poker face
No smile, no trace
Of hunger,
But your finger
Says danger
In a body language
And it is like a cage
That falls on your shoulder.
You mislead no one
With your old trap.
You are alone
With your road map
And you measure the gap
Between you and the younger.
You becomes older
For the game
That needs a big frame.
It's a shame.

Crime and Justice

Bonnie and Clyde

In 1930, Clyde Barrow was sentenced
To prison for fourteen years
That have been fenced
And without fears.
He did get paroled
In 1932, and in 1934 was holed
By Ted Hinton and five officers
In an ambush in Louisiana,
Near Gibsland
And the dicers
Very far from Montana,
And far also from Maryland,
Received more than fifty bullets
In the buffets.
In 1968, a film was shot by Arthur Penn
With Faye Dunaway as a star
Where sometimes we see a glen
And Warren Beatty and Gene Hackman.
Bardot with Gainsbourg, a musician
Created a song in memory of the spar.

Crammed Bag

Like the beavers
That build dams
On the rivers
To retain waters
You build scams
With some spams
To mislead credulous
And gentle suckers
That were sometimes truckers,
Promising a marvelous
And bright future,
With money in all nature.
You have a relative
That works as cashier, as country native,
In a big bank
At a high rank,
And she must put the old bank notes,
In order to burn them in big bags
But she fills her handy bags
With the small notes.

Customer Service

You go through customs.
In your right hand a pet
In the left hand, the daughter with a puppet.
There are seldom
Any controls
Nor any random
Patrols.
In the core
Of the puppet, cocaine,
And you can imagine
That no one will score
A father
With his child stuck together.
No one on the car park
No one in the night dark.
You take your vehicle,
In the glove compartment,
A pot of pickle,
But the boss waits in the apartment
With a tough element.

INMATES

Bernard Cadillon - *Inmate*

Jailhouse Tale

The children stretch
The arm
In the big farm
And they fetch
Their breath without harm
To catch the star
At the top of the fir,
Like behind the bar
A prisoner wanting to stir
A warder or an inmate
To try to change his fate,
But as for a merry Christmas
The presents are given
At the end of the mass.
The releases are gotten,
At the end when the crass
Becomes civilian and polite
And does not bite
Anymore
Even a sycamore

Italian Breaking

On the front page
You can read an homage
To your bravery
For the robbery,
Of the Mona Lisa
Painting
Also called Joconda
Before the opening
Of the Louvre museum,
At this time, before the first world war,
Not yet a kind of big aquarium,
In this time, when there were only a few car,
You entered and sounded the revenge
For the Italian compatriots,
All very patriots,
And you stole the portrait at your range.
Many years later,
Duchamp painted to Mona Lisa mustaches
With oil and not water
Giving to many headaches.

Jesse James

In 1847, came to world Jesse James.
As a teenager, he joined the Quandrill band
At the school of crime, he tames
Riots on the side of confederates. They stand
Following the war between the states.
He creates a gang on his own
That in the country constellates.
On January 1874 a train robbery
That has been shown
In so many western
Occurred in Gads Hill, not for a cranberry
10,000 dollars for the sterns.
In Piedmont, a posse was organized
But the James gang was sixty miles away
So they were unseized
And in 1881, he decided to pass away
But in 1882, in his home, he was shot
By a certain Robert Ford
However in the late 1940 an elder very hot
Claimed he was James, not hanged by a cord.

Miscarriage of Justice

"You were a rover,
But not a serial lover,
That had been jailed
For misdemeanours and an assault,
On a teenage girl that looked older.
You paid when you had failed,
But it was not your fault.
The girl was very attractive,
But now you must be talkative,
If you want to see your guilt diminished,
And that a plea bargain could be reached.
There is a rape and a murder,
It changes of gender.
What have you seen, what have you done?
Don't forget anyone,
Don't be mute,
If you want that we commute
Your sentence from death penalty
To life-time penalty."
And the poor guy confessed two crimes that seem
To have hurt his self-esteem,
Until the DNA analyses testify
That if he was crank
He was blank

Nuclear Spies

In August 1949, exploded the Russian bomb,
In 1953, the Rosenbergs were buried in tomb.
They belonged to the communist party,
It was the reign of Mac Carthy.
They were guilty.
No doubt, no casualty.
It was the witch hunt
Everyone was blunt.
For J. Edgar Hoover it was the century
Crime, and in the cemetery
They must rest.
To free them, the quest.
But they refuse to recognize
That, not in vain, they jeopardize
Their lives and their reputation.
No Manhattan project expectation.
For the enemy,
Killed only a dummy
And his wife, in no tradition
Of no transaction.

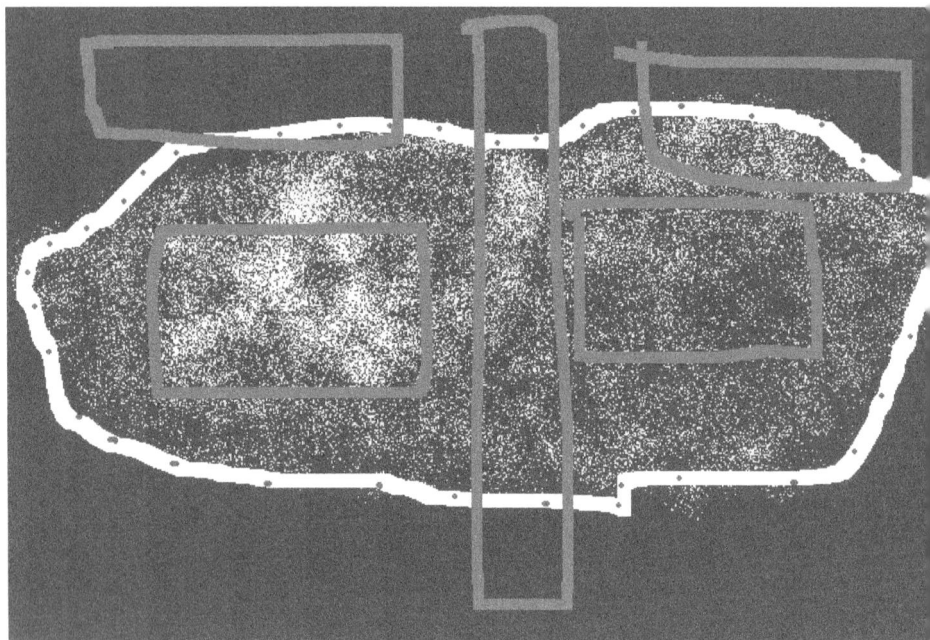

Bernard Cadillon - *Oyste*

Tutti Frutti

You ate tutti frutti
In Little Italy,
And tutti chianti,
Thinking "what a nice ice cream!",
Listening O Napoli.
Everyone was saying "Take it easy"
In the speak easy,
When you heard the scream
"One moment, only!"
Like the explosion of the Stromboli.
It came from a Mafioso
Praying padre doloroso,
In the sea food restaurant,
Where he ate scampi,
For just one Grant,
When the staccato
Of the bumpy
Gunfire started his concerto.
Like the other godfathers
He had found better weathers.

Rapist Therapist

You came from Romania or Hungary
You were hungry
Of the western hurry
You, that were so calm and peaceful
Sometimes very helpful,
Was actually a rapist,
Escaped from a hospital.
With the knowledge of the therapist,
That cured you with musical recital.
You passed some diploma
In psychology
To ease the trauma
Of the loss of analogy
With reality
And to maintain the mirror
Exempt of any error
In your behavior
And to give to each patient
The feeling to have a content
Worthy of the treatment.

Red Roses

You liked the Beatles,
And the whistles,
To appeal your victim
Sometimes a little dim.
You gave red roses
And your proses,
To Liz Koepfler,
But now you were taken in custody
Mister Ted Bundy.
As a lawyer,
You were self defender,
And even if you escaped twice,
You had no choice.
If you are not yet found guilty,
You are facing the death penalty,
And at the end of the drama,
You sat on yellow mama,
And measured the trauma
It is to burn in hell
Where you fell.

Know How

The witch has thrown her vow
On the gentle fellow,
That lives in the bungalow.
The black widow,
As most of the spiders,
Is of the poisonous genders.
She is more efficient
And silent
Than the bow and the arrow.
She steals by the window,
Hidden by the darkness below,
And she goes under the pillow.
The owner had received blackmail with a barrow,
Posted by a black crow,
But he did not pay attention
Of the notice and of the information.
Nothing to mention,
Except the assassination,
But without witnesses that he could know,
Except the children, swallowing his sorrow.

Cook Crook

The French cook
Was a crook.
He had made a cordon bleu cuisine
Read in a magazine,
And as the lady was skeptic,
Because she was a gastronomic critic
And that she found the sauce horrific,
He imagined dining in a fancy restaurant
Where they could pass an instant.
As he was a fancy man,
He stood not too distant,
Nevertheless the grand woman
Was not impressed by the kindness,
Because she remembered the tactless
Of his behavior,
And his timid endeavor
To pass his hand on his wrist
That she bent in a twist.
And having nothing to sell, nothing to buy,
She said bye-bye to the guy.

War

Beyond the War

Volver
And revolver.
One bullet in the barrel
For the scoundrel.
One shot in,
Five shots out,
You begin
And the others shout.
You are watching "deer hunter"
In the drive in
You pay at the counter
And you remember Vietnam
As a big sin
Against peace that Uncle Sam
Had perpetrated in the sixties
And that comes back
With other realities
In Iraq
Hopefully the American dream
Will continue with another team.

Feathered Warriors

Geronimo and Cochise
Were sitting
On their wounded knees
In the sunrise
Chatting
And trying
To foresee
What can be seen
On the mountain green.
A tomahawk
In his hand
A black hawk
On the land,
The feathered warrior
Finished his dance
Prior
To a trance
He looked at the Indian ridge
After the bridge
And then after
Indian summer

Virginia

Living in a cocoon
Born with a golden spoon
In the mouth
In the great south.
You had never seen a coon
Elsewhere than in the plantation
And never in his habitation,
So when the civil war
Began not far
From your homeland
Dreamt as a neverland,
It was a nightmare
That you had to share
With others as a white patron
To see tobacco and cotton
Fields left without caution
To the confederates
And to the northerners,
Not all desperate,
But often dead in the corners.

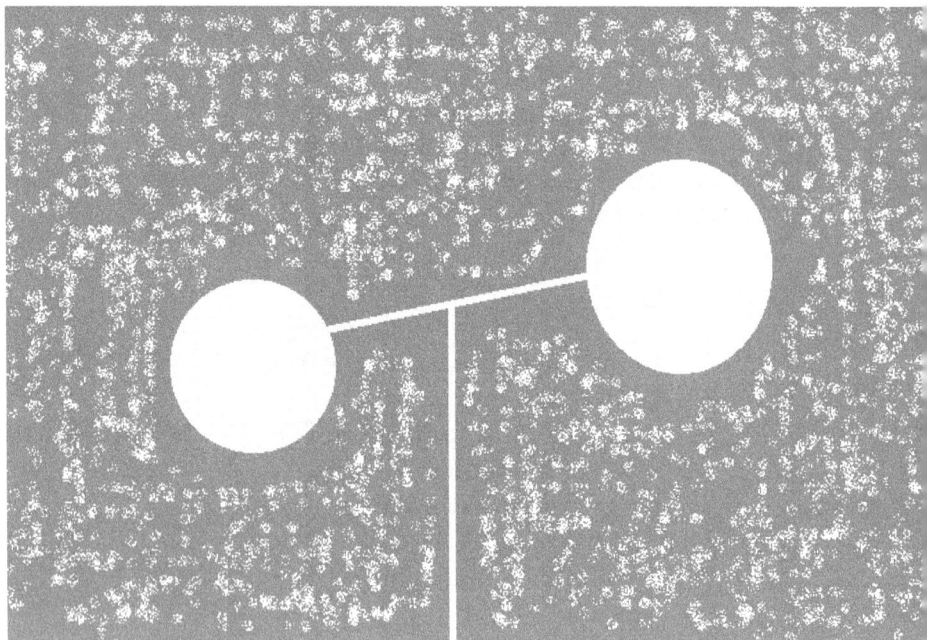

*Bernard Cadillon - **Anemomete***

Wind Talkers

You were smart
Before you start,
You ought to eat cod,
When you discover the code,
That was not Chinese,
That defied the Japanese.
In the name of your soul fathers,
You, that were born Indian American,
You betray your blood brothers,
But for the the ending of the wars,
In the Pacific ocean,
The stripes and stars
Banners had to float
On the islands and on your boat
You whistled
In silent titled,
Messages,
That were as new passages
Through the victory,
And the return to your sanctuary.

History

Bernard Cadillon - *Carria*

Bastille Day

You sit on the hedge,
You have given your heart
As a pledge
In the bottom of the cart.
You will be beheaded
At the end of the day.
Your beauty has faded
Away, no mercy, this Sunday
For a duchess.
You liked to play chess
But the bishop
Will kill the queen,
There is a stop.
The scaffold, at you have seen,
Is in place.
The guillotine in a large space
Will soon do its office.
From this bloody sacrifice
Of the French chivalry
Will emerge a new gentry.

Fisher-Spassky

The bishops follow the diagonal.
The chess-board is not octagonal
But square as for the draughts.
You have done a castling,
You have an advantage in the battling
And for the other fights.
And if you are not too slow,
You can imagine doing a checkmate
Before that it was too late.
The pawn will blow
The opposite queen
At what you have seen
At the last engagement.
Your competitor propose a drawn game.
You have to meditate
This new enlargement
That was not the same
That the one for which you hesitate
Till now to know
If it was defeat or window

Five Rings

The baron Pierre de Coubertin
Born in 1863, and of Norman origin
Was a sportsman very dynamic
That liked box, fencing
And was not really a comic.
He imagined creating
In 1894, new Olympic
Games with a committee,
And two years later,
In Athens as times flee,
The first Olympic game took matter.
In April 1915, were signed,
In the city hall of Lausanne,
Acts establishing an administrative center,
That lightened
The project that seemed insane
To restore a chivalry
Far from politics, conflicts and wars,
Where people could be merry,
From the five continents, without bars.

French Underground

You were in the maquis
Far from Paris
Not dressed in marquis
For the liberation
Of your country
That was an operation
Needing to try
All kinds of weapons
And after maybe pardons
For the inhabitants,
Not all resistants
You have a machine gun
Not at all for the fun.
Maybe it was a stern
Although there was no tern
In the neighbourhood,
Only a green wood.
The victory is near
Without fear
This time for good.

Lafayette et Rochambeau

From 1773 with the Boston Tea Party
To 1783 with the treaty of Paris
France has borne to the new country
Help and support to build new basis.
In 1780, a ship "l'Amazone"
With Vicomte de Rochambeau crossed the ocean
And no one was stone
That France tried to ban
United Kingdom to its colony.
It was not really felony.
In February 1781, the colonel Laurens
Was sent in France
To raise funds
For the new expeditions
And to make new bounds
And to obtain concessions
From England that brought
To the final battles
Of Saint-Kitts, in Antilles
And in Paris, to what they sought.

Los Alamos

Fleeing Germany and Mittle Europa
A lot of jewish brains
Came in America
To participate in the Manhattan project,
But everything remains
On the seal of secret,
Until "Little boy"
And "Fat man"
Detonated as a toy
With a red tan.
In three main
Laboratories improved the researches
In the physics domain
With Openheimer and Enstein
As the heads of the arches.
It was the first steps.
We were only to the A bomb
At Los Alamos, full of peps.
Only Teller imagined a superbomb
Premiss of the hydrogen bomb

Mach 2

In 1971, a white bird, as told
Called Concorde; a bold
Technological challenge
And in a certain extend a revenge
For old Europa
On America;
Came into the world.
After a moment the cold
War obliged Russian
To build a Tupolev, pale imitation.
Like a boeotian,
But the frustration
Will not last very long,
Because 1978 song
The end of this supersonic.
Nevertheless in avionic
Science the wheel turns
And in 2000, Concorde burns
In a crash
That made tremendous clash.

Nacht und Nebel

The red driver
Was not a diver,
But he was the architect
Of the final solution,
That was the reflect
Of a foolish conception
Of world and humanity,
With lords and slaves
And no community
Except in the raves
Of a great Germany,
That never existed
As a harmony,
Even for musicians quoted.
Ricardo Clemente was his nickname,
But his real name
Was more sinister
And can be found on some register.
For him no tomb, no grave,
That rest gave.

The Lost Generation

Was born in 1874, Gertrude Stein
In Pittsburgh, Pensylvania.
She was the daughter of a Jewish origin
Industrial of California.
She grew up in Europa
At four years of age,
She came back to America
But only for a passage.
In 1902, in Paris, although conservative
She defended modern art.
She liked to create controversia
In the salon where she was talkative.
Between 1906 and 1908, she wrote a smart
Failure book "the making"
That in 1925, finally was published.
She was stalking
For the autobiography
That established
Her as a stenography
And a painting authority.

The Two Canals

Ferdinand de Lesseps, a French diplomat,
Born in 1805 had links
With the son of the Egyptian king.
In these times no combat,
In 1854, the king dead, he thinks
To projects that ting
In the ears of the young sovereign.
On the isthmus, he managed the campaign
That lasted ten years,
From 1859 to 1869 with some fears
For the delays,
But inaugurated at the normal days.
Ten years later, in Panama,
A company was created,
But the climate and the elements defeated
His ambition and gave trauma
To the shareholders,
That were not all elders,
And he escaped hardly
To the jail and died cowardly.

Twin Statues

A French sculptor
Called Bartholdi
In many ways inventor
Except for melody,
That was Alsatian
And not boetian
Knew the glory
Beyond the History,
Creating the statue of Liberty
Later than Jules Verne's editor, Pierre-Jules Hetzel
And with the help of an engineer, Gustave Eiffel,
That built bridges and a tower,
Working with their craftmen
They made the draft of the two women.
The big one is the gift of France,
In all sincerity,
To commemorate the independence
Of the great power,
With her torch lightening humanity.
One is in New York
In stone and not in cork,
On Ellis Island.
The other one in Paris,
Hidden on a little island,
And only seen by photo safaris.

White Bird

The Spirit of Saint-Louis
Few under the arch of triumph
In 1927, in Paris
Giving birth
To a myth.
It was the first time
That someone crossed
North Atlantic in prime,
Once and without stops.
By fortune tossed,
Four years later, the cops
Caught a kidnapper
That was called Hauptmann
That was a carpenter,
But not a harper,
And of German
Origin and lineage
But that had killed
The child Lindbergh, young in age,
And so on yellow mama grilled.

Revolution

(Variant of Bastille day)

You sit on the hedge
You have given your heart
As a pledge
At the bottom of a cart.
You will be beheaded
At the end of the day.
Your beauty has faded
Away, no mercy, this Sunday
For a duchess
.You liked to play chess
But the pawn
Will kill the queen,
Frightened as a prawn.
The scaffold at you have seen
Is in place.
The guillotine in a large space
Will soon do its office.
From this bloody sacrifice
Of the French chivalry
Will emerge a new gentry.

Sixty-nine, Eighty-nine

Sixty-nine, the year after,
The worldwide revolution,
Life was softer
"You tell me it's an evolution",
In this decade, sang the Beatles.
The dances, the trance
The demonstrations, the battles,
Berkeley in America, Nanterre in France.
After the great masquerades
The barricades,
The friendship, the comrades.
"The times, they are a changing"
Sang Bob Dylan,
Still gipsy and bohemian
The future, imagining,
Eighty-nine, twenty years later,
Le Mur de Berlin has fallen,
Somehow for a better
World, with no more liberty stolen.

Music

Family Rock

Mum
Plays drum
Marcello
Plays cello
Adriano
Plays piano
Marylin
Plays violin
Carola
Plays viola
Edgar
Plays guitar
And all together, they rock
Around the clock,
Clockwise
Anticlockwise

Spanish

Mariposa

Mariposa, Mariposa
Mi esposa,
Camina
Bajo la luna
Rosa
Mariposa, Mariposa
Mi esposa
Se quema
Hasta el alma
Bajo el sol ardiente
Y tan caliente.
Mariposa, Mariposa
¿Qué queda
De tu vuelo
Hasta el cielo?
Tu mirada,
Tan misteriosa
Y tan hermosa.

French

Iambe Ingambe

Si la césure à l'hémistiche
Lasse c'est sur l'amie, triche
Mais préfère à la libre
La rime riche
Qui engendre moins de quiproquo
Que tous les avatars du sexe aequo
Qui satisfont pourtant la fibre
Des vantards du rock coco.
Sache qu'un homme fort lit l'ode
Parfois sans folie, sans méthode
Qu'il a composé pour sa muse
Sans que jamais ne s'amuse
La belle, que soixante-neuf
Ne sonne jamais après Gracchus Babeuf ;
La bête à deux dos
Nécessite de la femme l'endos
Et de l'homme le vit sans repos
Perçant la lune
Brune
Après un Rossini tournedos.

Poupée Russe

Je jouais à la roulette russe
Pendant que tu terminais ta salade russe
Avant le dessert
Dans le cabaret désert.
Je faisais le solo
Et toi le chorus,
Du côté de Picpus,
Ainsi va la chanson, a volo,
A capella.
Devant la pizza avec la mozarella,
Que j'avais achetée avec tes emprunts russes,
On mangeait des blenis
Après avoir vu les ballets russes,
Glisser sur les parquets vernis
De l'Opéra de Paris.
On changea à Chaussée d'Antin
Et tu dormis avec ton pantin,
Moi avec ma poupée russe,
Dans le lit gigogne,
En buvant un bourgogne.

Présumés Innocents

Les gibiers de potence
Demandent l'indulgence
Et même la clémence
Pour leur méfaits;
Les vêtements défaits
La mine patibulaire,
Le regard circulaire,
Ils attendent d'être jugés
Mais ne sont pas insurgés
Devant les verdicts
Qui attendent les convicts.
C'est très moche
De faire les poches
De ses proches,
Et même cloche
Quand on s'accroche
Avec anicroche
Sous le porche
Avec un gendarme
Peut être de Parme.

Prosodie

Ton silence était éloquent,
Même un peu grandiloquent.
Tu aimais les oxymores,
Autant que les sycomores,
Sur les chemins
Qui mènent à Rome
Si l'on trouve le palindrome
En lisant les parchemins
Qui relient Sees à Laval,
Sur les traces de Cheval
Et de ses sculptures
Presque grandeurs natures.
Métaphore, métonymie,
Cent fusils
Pour l'accalmie,
Cent poudres de barils.
Enfin tout est serein et tranquille
Comme une petite fille
Qui tourne l'aiguille
Comme une anguille.

Show Business

A Streetcar Named Brando

After some trials in Broadway
He started with Elia Kazan really
In A streetcar named Desire.
It is during a play
That he fighted badly
With a scene-shifter in fire.
At the Actors Studio, with the help of Stella Adler
He developed a new interpretation
And in 1973, with "the Godfather"
Won his second Oscar,
That he refused to show his opposition
To the way the war
With Indians in exhibition
Were treated in movies
Behind the cameras, he has once been
For one eyed jacks as a director
But he has made little studies
For this western out of screen.
He appears the last time as actor
In the score, when clinks the peen

Citizen Welles

In 1941, at twenty six years old,
He broadcasted Citizen Kane
But it was not his first endeavour.
He had worked for the radio, bold
Adaptations of plays,
And crane
scenario of Macbeth in favour
Of a transfer as clays
To Tahiti with black actors
Not of these sectors.
For his first film, the critic
Was unanimous,
But the audience was not dramatic.
He was nevertheless famous
With his second film, the same
Thing, but he expected that audience came.
With the fourth film Gilda, only
The success arrived mainly.
In France, in 1958, he met André Bazin
With whom he made an interview on Eisenstein.

Elvis

King
He was
Far from jazz.
In the ring
In Las Vegas
Late in the sixties
"Love me tender"
And "Jailhouse rock"
Were the ties,
Not "Return to sender"
That was in stock,
With success
And his come back
Was in progress,
For each cheap jack
Capacity to sell million
Of black disks
Of the great lion
Without risks.

His Way

Claude François had written
A song called « Comme d'habitude »
That was the message
From a man to his maiden
Full of latitude
In almost all the passage.
Paul Anka heard him playing
In Paris and he decided
To adapt the displaying
Text in English figured,
And it became "My way"
Interpreted by numerous
Of brilliant crooners
Pure as at midway,
And so fabulous
That in the sooners
Or in the laters
All the starters
Try to fish after compliment
With their voices as implement.

Jules and Joe

For the MGM, Jules Dassin
Begins with Nazi agent
In the forties
Far from Eisenstein,
But blacklisted, for all intent
To survive in the fifties,
He fled to France
Where he realized in good stance
A great film of gangsters
With murders in the roasters.
His son Joe after acting
The second knife
In some of his plays
Decided to start singing
And he adapted in a way naïve
Standards and a song that stays
In the seventies as "the hit"
The success and the honor split
With Delanoe a songmaker highly lit
And "the Albatross" a tight fit

Limelights

In 1914, Charlot appears as the first
Character of a long list
Of films and movies.
In 1916, he signs a contract
That gives hives,
Because one million dollar
Was the tract,
Longtime before the blue collar
In Modern Times
With oil and grimes,
That was the last mute
Film with no flute.
In 1940, The Great Dictator
Was broadcasted in each sector
Of the western countries
Will follow other sceneries
Notably with the help of Welles
For Monsieur Verdoux at the finales
Criminal in the crackles
Beheaded as Landru and other models.

The Tonkinese

In june 1906, Saint-Louis gave birth
To Josephine Baker
Born Freda Josephine Mac Donald
That found a path
In France before Charlie Parker.
In 1925, she danced bald.
She became the muse
Of the cubists, that the revues fuse.
In 1931, she sang a melody
"J'ai deux amours" of Vincent Scotto
That the words embody
In the tone legato
Her love for Paris, her new country
And for America, her fatherland.
In 1937, she did not belong to the gentry
But she gained French citizenship
And in 1947, imagined a neverland
Where orphans could live in friendship,
But ruined, she went into exile
In Monaco; adopted without any bile.

.

Sport

Edith and Marcel

He was a boxer French.
He was born in Morocco,
But he was white as a trench
In the wind sirocco,
Because his colleagues
Of the boxing leagues
Were black in most of the case
And sometimes Arabic, on the base
Of the athletic origin,
Quality that had surged in
The belt owner.
He was a bomber,
His name was Cerdan, the champ,
His lover was Piaf, the singer,
And at his death with a cramp
She composed the "hymne a l'amour"
That was a sour
Appeal in favour
Of her beloved hero, unburied
For ever, in the sky disappeared.

Madison Square Garden

You wander the streets,
Happy go lucky,
But no one to meet,
Fool but not wacky.
You, that was the great boxing champ,
Is now a poor tramp.
You lost your vision
After the last round,
Where they have found
You without any reason.
You beg the passers-by,
For mercy
Or for pity,
If they are not on stand-by,
To give you a penny,
Hiding your gold medal,
In so precious metal,
To your past deny.

Various

911

Hang on
Hold on
Hold the line
Until your pains shine.
I pass my life on the phone
Answering to people stone.
You are a drug addict,
I am a work addict
I can solve a conflict
My little Benedict
If you give me a piece
Of information
On your fears and your caution,
No money, no specie.
Are you a junky
And do you find it funky.
What is your occupation?
Does it give you satisfaction?
Are you a bread earner
Or the wife of a mariner?

Big Shot

The former Robin Hood
In his childhood
Used to fight the villain.
In vain, in vain.
He is now a big shot,
Not very hot.
Maybe a short person,
Surely a square person.
He looks up each Monday
The prices of his shares
But has nothing to share.
Sometimes he says mayday,
But quickly finds the way.
He is a great tycoon
In his honeymoon,
Happily married
With a Lady Mary,
A kind of Bill Gates,
But with closed gates.

Bless You

The computer you harness
After he played chess
Cried "press"
The button madness
"God you bless
You find the fitness
After the dryness.
A bug, I guess.
Nevertheless
I'll check if no mess
As I confess
In a coolness
Let the core topless
Or bottomless.

Bohemian Burgess

From the ceiling
To the cellar,
You must tidy
And make the dusting
Of the table for brandy.
On the desk in cedar,
Suddenly unveiling,
The Marylin calendar,
In which she posed naked.
Nothing peculiar,
Except the painting unpacked,
On the floor,
Near the door.
All the furniture are vintage,
Except the desk, for the advantage
Of the visitors
That are not all inspectors.
In the bar, food and beverage,
On the wall, a flying sausage,
Unidentified Flying Object,
That was a good discussion subject.

Boon Cartoons

You enjoy yourself very much
Seeing cartoons such
As the wolf and the ginger
Of Tex Avery, you laughed a lot,
When you heard Woody woodpecker,
Making more noise than a pneumatic drill,
In all the plot,
Efficiently brill.
Tom running
After Jerry,
In a way so cunning,
That they leave us merry.
Popeye the sailor,
With his spinach box,
That gives him great valor,
To fight like a fox.
Each time, for us, it was comic trips
Sometimes like in the comic strips,
But as Bugs Bunny says when he talks,
"That's all folks".

Burning Hot

Scarcely rare
Is my steak.
Do you speak
English and do you care
What I say
Or is it just an essay?
In the middle
It is medium
Creaking as a fiddle
For the criterium,
And on the top
Maybe it is pop
But surely well done
As in a cone.
Do you have French mustard
Mister steward?
No we have the English one.
Has the new waitress gone?
No. As usual white coffee
With mint and a toffee.

Call Center

You work for call center
Whose supervisor data conveys
You make polls and surveys
On lodgers and renters.
Behind you, on the desks
Telephones and computers.
Nobody takes risks.
You have a contract
For each filled questionnaire.
It is not abstract,
To be millionaire
You have to catch
Of the listeners, the attention,
And to patch
With caution
All of their objections
For all the situations,
And in ten minutes to know
What are their surfaces now.

Colors

Blue
As a clue
Red
As the bread
Yellow
As the mellow
Brown
As the town
Black
As the stack
White
As the bite
Green
As the spleen
Orange
As the change
Violet
As the toilet.

Crash Test

You are on the highway.
You exceed
The speed.
No one to sway.
To you, no one on the bypass,
So you can go fast.
No crowd, no mass
Until the last
Junction.
You have only to pay attention
To the fuel in your tank,
It is Wednesday, you can be crank,
But suddenly, coming from nowhere,
A woman, with her daughter,
At your right, you drift on your left,
Where there was no one there,
Except a youngster
That wanted as a gift
To go to the jeweler
To buy a ring to his bride
Whom he could take pride.

Delicatessen

I am in heaven
Said the raven
In the garden
I am in heaven
Said the maiden
In the kitchen
I am in heaven
Said the chicken
In the oven
I am in heaven
Smiled the children
Very often
I am in heaven
Sang the abdomen
In the delicatessen

Divorce

No matter what,
No matter who.
It's up to date,
It's up to you
… Or you love me,
Or I leave you.
It's up to date,
It's up to you
… Or you see me,
Or I sue you,
It's up to date,
It's up to you
… So frenchkiss me
If I miss you.
It's up to date,
It's up to you
Or you call me,
Or I phone you
It's up to you.

Bernard Cadillon - Swimming poo

Dream in Blue

You started up a blue ship
After the blue trip
That you made on a blue field
In Nicaragua,
Near its capital Managua,
In central America.
As a shield,
You subscribed a loan
With your friend Soan.
As a borrower, with no ban
You had made a business plan
And you will commence
Reimbursing the capital
In two years for the essential,
And the rest at your convenience.
When your balance sheet,
According to the accounting science,
Will balance,
And that your feet
Will be on the same sheet.

Doctor Freud

-Hello Doctor,
I would like to explain
To you in what nightmare
I have fallen with the inspector...
-The same that did not care
Neither the starter, nor the main
-Exactly, and what did he obtain?
-To see you again and again
-You are a magician.
-No, I am just a physician.
-And what is your analysis
Of my crisis?
-Give me a slice of your brain
That I could retain.
-We were in a pub, and he ordered elephant,
And he saw me laughing,
He pressed the ring,
And all the waiters ran in an instant
And I woke up quickly
-Breaking your dream eternally.

Drive Me Crazy

Take the U turn
Slowly
Or you will get upside down
And the car will burn
Badly
As on the picture shown
What a screwy idea
You have with your nausea
To go for a lift
Reading Swift
That is difficult to understand
As mentioned on the cover
Of the book in your hand
A short time to recover
Will be necessary
Fortunately the car is undamaged
And you have changed
Of place and the starry
Sky can prove as a testimony
That you would rest in harmony.

Faithful

Slim
As a muslim
Alcoholic
As a catholic
Hesitant
As a protestant
Selfish
As a jewish
Childish
As an amish
According to your faith
You find your path
In the jungle
And in the bible.
You commit a sin
Sometimes too thin
That your attention
Could mention.

Fashion Victim

Do what you want !
Wear a skirt Mary Quant
If you dare
To be the nightmare
Of the look of the old fashion
With the new collection,
But leave my tattoo,
My tattoo is taboo.
It is a gift of a lover
That was a remover
At the end of our affair
That he found unfair.
It is like a jewellery
Shining as a silvery
Fox
Escaped of his box.
Go to the mannequin parade
And find the charade.
The designer dressed extravagantly
Or the tailor ignorant permanently.

French Heritage Society

French Heritage Society
Is an association
That fights with fidelity
To preserve the construction
And the improvement of the link
Between France and America
And specially in Louisiana
Before that the elements sink
The town in calamity
Without any amenity.
It has chapters in France
And in United States
Where some dependence
Impulse the debates
And the restoration
And the decoration
Of old castels
And old mansions
Sometimes with colors pastels
And in great dimensions.

Getaway

Waiting for the minestrone
You look at each milestone
To see if your wreck
Could reach the deck
Without damage
Except your rampage.
You will atone
Your sins, alone
Near the cone
Of Corcovado
Or at Montevideo.
The blades shone,
You watch each bone
To see if the skeleton
Could bear you till Boston.
You have a wound
But you have found
A surgeon
That could prevent it to burgeon
Unless you were the next pigeon.

Globe Trotter

In Ulan Bator, I search the big mogul
I eat turkey in Istanbul
I break china in Beijing
I wear a panama on the canal
In india, I taste Darjeeling,
In Australia, I jump as a marsupial.
In Stockolm, I walk on blue suede shoes,
But the owner, a Scottish, had toes
In bad shape for a dancer,
So I received a jab
In Thai boxing.
I threw him a saucer,
In return he gave me a little dab.
I did not know if he was foxing
And I smile
Thinking at the mile
Between the theater and my car
That I could not reach with an Oscar,
Because of my pain and the scar
That left me as a tartar.

Identification

What is your name ?
Your last name !
Cadillon
Like Cadillac but with on
And your first name?
Bernard
As a bear hard
And your stage-name?
Benny
When it's sunny.
And your nickname?
Nanard
Same as canard.
It's the French name
Of duck.
Give me a buck
And I'll tell you
What is a voyou
If you want to compromise
Yourself, you won't jeopardize,
So call me frenchy.
It's my citizen name
And it sounds like friendship
That is not a word but a name.

In Vitro

You were a student
No more adolescent
Needing money
For your new honey
And you imagine
To give your spermatozoon
Nine months will be soon
To a nice and genuine
Girl maybe Italian.
You are not grey
As you say
And are a Swedish American.
Your code number
Is sixty six as the highway,
But twenty years later
Your unknown daughter
Clever as a tumbler
Gave a name to her father
And even without heritage
Can now have a lineage.

Incunabulum

In the library
You are looking for an incunabulum
Hidden by an album
Of weapons and military
Soldiers and an uncomplimentary
Book that burns
Like some trees
At farhenheit 451 degrees.
The author was Ray Bradbury.
The librarian searches and turns
At the corner of the shelf.
"Please yourself".
It is no more time of tilbury
Speed and hurry
Impose the end
Of the Galaxy Gutenberg.
It is the trend
Sad as the death of Jean Seberg
And the suicide of Romain Gary
A French writer extraordinary.

India

To visit the subcontinent,
It is not the right moment,
But you can have a clear vision
Of the devastation
Watching television
Or chatting
Or speaking
With the Indian
Inhabitants.
Go to the restaurant
You will smell the kind of combo
That you can eat in Colombo.
Take the salt
For your curry
And malt
Or Bloody Mary.
Many miles worth
To the north
Taste Darjeeling
And give me your feeling.

Jet Set

Because of the generation gap
You have a top lap
And your father
In the park lane
A big computer
That it is difficult to hide
In the airplane,
Even in the back side.
On your seat, you take a drink
And on the web, search a link,
Because of the jet lag,
You were tired
And near to be fired,
So, you must find a new jet flag,
To be back home
At time for the wedding,
But still handsome,
At the seeming.

Landlord

You have a tough
Cough,
You snore through
The door.
Poor, poor
Landlord.
You dream
To be in the cream.
Landlord, landlord,
But you sleep in a slum.
You belong to the scum.
It seems creepy to see where you live,
In hell, you dive.
Each night you swim
Against streams
Each so dim,
But in the morning
You have plenty of steams,
That look corning.

Mady

Oh, my dear, my dear, my dear Mady
You were so nice, you were so cute
That I felt really unsecured
Oh my dear, my dear, my dear Mady
You were the one of your kind
You were the one in my mind
Oh my dear, my dear, my dear Mady
I must confess that you were the greatest
I have ever boasted
Oh my dear my dear my dear Mady
I liked black coffee
But I have not paid the fee
Oh my dear my dear my dear Mady
You remember my name
I remember your fame
Oh my dear my dear my dear Mady
You played the game
Without any shame
Oh my dear my dear my dear Mady
You were so nice, you were so cute
That I felt really rude.

Monkey Donkey

On the same road
Walked a monkey
And a grey donkey.
After living abroad,
They came back
In their village.
Looking at the big smoke-stack,
In their own language,
They tried to comfort
That they will soon drop in the port,
That things were going on.
Confident, they had carried on
Their path to a great jamboree,
But a circus searched a chimpanzee.
They caught the little animal,
And wanted to harness in the coral
The quadruped
But the donkey kicked
And tricked
The lads on the fence
And they found his defence
Supernatural
As these of an insightful animal
And freed them in a manner exceptional

New Comer

You change of topics,
You change of tropics
With Henry Miller
And sometimes Sallinger.
You change of matters
After the Masters,
You remember the twin Williams
And their fabulous slams.
It is also America
Dreamed maybe in Santa Monica.
In cold blood,
You speak with Capote,
In cold mood
To what you devote
And he answers on a cloud round
Reading, maybe Ezra Pound
A making a little bound
On earth, to land,
In hell, to stand.

New London

Are you Irish ?
No I am British.
Do you take the highway
When you go on holiday?
No I take the motorway.
During the week do you take the subway?
No, I take the underground
At the end of the round.
I leave my car at the parking lot
Where there are a lot.
Mine stays at the car-park
Near Hyde Park.
And downtown,
Is there a roundabout,
Or only in the villages round about.
In my town,
In the city center
No one can enter,
Because it is a pedestrian street
Where people together meet.

New Orleans

If you send a résumé
I presume
That he will be digest
For the best.
If you give a glance
In France,
By chance
A wizard
Can give you a regard.
Don't exaggerate,
And don't use
The world abuse
If you are late.
If you want to thank
Someone by pity
Don't say mercy
Specially at the first rank.
Some people have bad temper
But they are not always "a character".
.

Nice, France

Nice, France
Two belovers sought
What they thought
Could be a paradise
Hidden in the sunrise
In the south of France
For a romance
They were in the middle
Of their lives
They have passed to the riddle
All the proposals,
Some were so naive
And at their disposal
A brochure
On the Riviera culture
Love at first sight
Love at first night
Love at first fight
Love at first flight
Love for ever
Love not fever.

Nightly Gardening

You wanted to help an ex convict
That was a drug addict
And you engaged him as a gardener
And maybe as a sparing partner.
"Is today
The D-day
Is tonight
The D-night"
Song the youngster.
"After diner
You took a supper,
Opening my purse cord"
Replies the land lord,
The gentleman farmer called his lawyer
Because the sawer
Had cut the wrong branch
In the ranch.
He is now in a sorry plight
He is really in a sorry light.
No power, no energy
Nothing very sunny.

Now

The slow shadow
Near the bow window
Blew a name
And "Tomorrow"
And when "Tomorrow"
Came
The slow shadow
Blew "Now"
In the white snow
And the man fell down
Upside down
Because now
Was his name.

Odyssey

In the Mediterranean sea, so vast,
Ulysse, bound to his mast,
Could not hear the mermaid
On the sand laid,
Singing without delay
Her melancholic melodies
And sometimes the replay,
That entered by the ears in the bodies
Of the sailors
That were not traitors,
But that had no wax
To collapse the sound of the sax
And of the skipper
That had to do the wiper
Between the reefs, in the creek,
That was, in this time greek.
Finally he succeeded to fill the pipe
Of these resonant organs, and to let the men go for a dip
When they reached the shore
Crying "Never More".

On Stage

It is the best book-shop
For the drama
Comma,
Said the bishop
Full stop.
If you like theater
You will find some matter.
The spirit of Shakespeare
Does not expire
Without rage
On stage.
Read the front page
Of each play
And see what authors lay
On the manuscripts
And sometimes on the tapuscripts,
As thank
To this think tank

Poetry.com

You have a brand new computer
That passed muster
At the first look.
You have access to internet
And that took
Only a few minutes
To change of planet
With a signature tune of lutes
You surf on a website
Specialised on poetry,
You hesitate
But you finally find an entry
Bernard was the first name
Cadillon was the last name
The poetry was "shadows".
It contains sorrows,
It starts with a verse
Separated at the hemistich
It finishes at the converse
By something not mobbish.

Pregnant

-Do you like fruits ?
-Have you suits ?
Eat strawberries
-We have only blueberries
I prefer blackberries
-What to speak of cranberries
Forget the berries
I have other queries
-Do you take the ferries
When you go on holiday
Because each day
You eat cherries.
It may be risky
For your foetus
With all your whisky
During the oestrus
To have an abortion
In high proportion.
Listen chorus
But avoid asparagus

Rich Dish

The Scottish fish
Has been captured
In the place he ventured
Near the Spanish beach
That he finally succeeded to reach.
He had garish
Colors
That finished to abolish
After hours
Of fighting.
The garlic bread
Will be used as garnish
With his head
And a lemon lighting.
In the parish
All the people know
Now
That the fish has perished
And has not vanished.

Safe Way Home

Have a safe journey back
Listening Paint it black
Have a nice day
Listening Billie Holiday
Have a safe journey home
Listening C.Jerome
So on, so on
Listening Jim Morrison
See you soon
Listening Dark side of the moon
So long, so long
Listening Tai Phong
Take the free way
Listening Cab Calloway.
Enjoy your diner
Listening Gardiner.
Buy me a drink
Listening Pink
So on, so on,
Locomotion

Sand, Sea, Sun

In a desert
There is a bordello
Where eating a dessert
You can hear Elvis Costello
In a oasis
There is an inn
Where you can hear Janis Joplin
Under the picture of Onassis.
In palm groves
There is a lounge
Where you can here rock grunge
And everybody moves
Waiting for the construction
Of a new resort
And the abduction
Of a new sort
Of Sabrina
By a rider
That as a spider
Searched a marina

Speak Easy

When a blue collar
Meets a white collar
What are they talking about?
Of the colour of the collar
Drinking one stout
After another
And steaming with a cigar
When it does not bother
Them to feel the smoke
And to receive a stroke
Because the trade-unionists
If they don't like communists
Don't like above all
Blacklegs
And when they fall
As some bootlegs
On bad whisky
It can be risky
For the black sheep
To find the big sleep.

Stardust Memories

You were drinking tea with lime
Just behind the mime
Sparkling the limelights
In the darkness of the nights.
Your morning mouth
Was opened in Bournemouth.
There were the grey clouds
So loud.
All the timetables
Proved that you were unable.
There was the Battistini
And there was Christiani.
Catering is a hard job
Even if you are a child of the art
Playing darts.
Like everyone, you have forgotten
But not forgiven
All the forgeries that were given
And although he was not an alien
All the waiters were waiting for Bob.

Start Up

At the age to be pink
You were punk,
You listened Johnny Rotten
When you were kitten
But now you have gotten
The award
For your life of bard
And a producer
Also good inducer
Persuaded you to record
A song on an album
And each cord
Of the bass
And the beat of the drum
Gather the mass
At your concerts
Far from the deserts
Of the first audiences
Where the obediences
To the fashion created defences.

Suicide by Cops

You take your gun
For fun
You hold the wheel
In your car,
How do you feel
Fine, without a scar.
In the police academy, today
And at this moment
Only youngsters
Trying to flay
Without comment
Grow up gangsters.
You turn on the left, on the right
As a drunk for a fight.
The patrol follows
You, with full light
No pains, no sorrows.
Yours eyes still opened
But your gun shows
Your wish to be corned.

Temping Agency

"You are not a good secretary,
You make too much discrepancies,
For any of our agencies,
Even if your contract is temporary.
You type with two fingers,
As can do absolute beginners.
You are computer literate
As I am your school-mate.
You live in your fancy
World, but eat in fancy
Restaurants, that no one can afford,
Except a Lady or a Lord.
Yesterday, you were drunk
As a skunk.
You do not pay attention
To the details, nor to the mention,
In the margin,
At the origin
Of the letter,
That was put by the writer."

The Fallen Tycoon

The tycoon
Lay on his back
Completely taken aback
By the crossing of the typhoon
Even if he was the one husband
Dead on the sand
Everyone was dumb
Was he murdered
As some whispered.
There was a strange stain
On his limb
As the rolling of a train
Everyone was awake
But if there was a mistake
No tears went by
Even by and by
And on the grave in the marble
Was put the emphasis
On a permanent basis
That he was brave and able

Translator, Traitor

For the italian
As for the American
"Traduttore
Traditore",
Has the same meaning,
That needs the caning.
It signifies translator,
Traitor.
Because you can not give the genius
Of a tongue, and its continuous
Progressive learning,
Each morning,
Eating croissant,
Drinking coffee,
For the first instant
Of the day, before the toffee.
And even if you have travelled a lot
And been involved in each plot
As a spy or a journalist,
Sometimes, you need a list.

Trick Dicky

The hooker
Stood on his heel
Played snooker
And, all they feel
That it was not the game
For which his fame
Could be spread
And be read
On all the continents
And for all the commitments
He put the balls
In the holes
But the calls
Were not for his soles
Nor for his behavior
That was of a traitor,
Because his feet
Were not always on the ground
And you can meet
Him on each round

Twelve Elves

You wander
On the yonder
Hill and you wonder
If there were elves
And if they were the twelves.
Nevertheless the holy spirit
In despite
Of the tense
Used the preterite
To speak with a sprite
In a manner so intense
That the poor little mite
That was standing
On the painting
In the haunting
Chapel, fell down
Of the frame brown.
The vicar
Scared, but not liar
Gave him a dollar.

Wild West

In the morn
The cow broke a horn
On the barbed wire
And the driver
As a hire
Received a staple in silver.
The lawn was shorn
But so dry was set on fire
And the curtain was torn.
Guilty was the little mire.
He ate sweet corn
Thinking to the pip
In his life and of the tip
That he could receive
If he did not deceive
The landlord
That can afford
To pay a lad
And to lie glad
That another was on the cord

Zebras

Zebra crossing
No trespassing
Stop
Zebra crashing
No trespassing
Walk
Zebra crushing
No trespassing
Drop
Zebra rushing
No trespassing
Talk
Zebra brushing
No trespassing
Lop.

Zoo

In the park, the zebra
Looked at the woman
With a wonderbra
Near the pond
Rich of caiman.
The baboon
That she found
So boon
Drew her camera.
The boy sang a De Valera
Poem and the monkey
Fled away.
On the lake, she rented a boat.
With her stentorian
Voice, Mary shouted "An alligator, Yan"
And the zingaro opened the throat
Of the toothed animal
And put a truncheon
To avoid with this vegetal
To become a good luncheon.

Bernard Cadillon

Bournemouth Hotel

(variant of Stardust Memories)

You were drinking tea with lime
Just behind the mime
Sparkling the limelights
In the darkness of the nights
Your morning mouth
Was opened in Bournemouth
There were the grey clouds
So loud
But the timetable
Proved that you were an able
There was the Battistini
And there was Christiani.
Catering is a hard job.
Even if you are a child of art
Playing darts
Like everyone you have forgotten
But not forgiven
All the forgiveness that were given
And although he was not an alien
All the waiters were waiting for Bob.

Interconnection

-Are you the switchboard operator?
-No, I am the receptionist
-I am a tour operator,
A little bit hedonist,
Who can I introduce?
-John Bruce
-I'll put you through
To the general manager,
If you are less tough.
-Apologize my anger,
But I am in a hurry
Because my schedule
Can not admit any delay,
And I would be very sorry,
If, because of your scruples,
I could not transmit the relay.
-Do not worry,
The general manager will ease your pain,
And I am sure that a lot you can earn again,
If you light his brain.

www.ingramcontent.com/pod-product-compliance
Lightning Source LLC
LaVergne TN
LVHW051639080426
835511LV00016B/2393